THE LIGHT OF STARS LONG CEASED TO BE

First published in 2025
by Eyewear Publishing, an imprint of
The Black Spring Press Group
Grantully Road, Maida Vale, London W9,
United Kingdom

Cover design and typeset by Edwin Smet

ISBN 978-1-917788-60-1

BLACKSPRINGPRESSGROUP.COM

**Judge's Citation, Christopher Jackson,
The Melita Hume Poetry Prize**

Pugh's poetic world is a place where human insight is linked irrevocably to far-off galaxies – it is a book which attempts to come to terms with the enormity of the universe by creating a large inner imaginative space. It does so by sourcing in confident language the "inconsolable ebb" of the universe – as if something true has been fetched from the other side of the universe, and found expression here. Their book is a realisation that patterns out there may have some relevance here, where we face our political reckonings (in a "Rotten Nationalist America") and our injustices, or "the Machiavellian misogynistic masochism", as Pugh calls it. In spite of its large temporal and spatial ambitions, it is also a book for our time.

THE LIGHT OF STARS LONG CEASED TO BE

WHYT PUGH

THE BLACK SPRING PRESS GROUP

This book is dedicated to my sister, Nessie Leigh Knoll, who died shortly after her 20th birthday. She appears on the cover as the archetypal representation of the Seven Sisters of the Pleiades. I shot the photograph with a 5x4 box camera on the bank of the American River, not far from where she was born. The cosmic thread of the collection is made evident by the Fibonacci spiral pouring from her hands, embedding stone and space in one and other as the images of the poems do. She is the figure of The Dead Girl who features in "Blodeuwedd," "Still Life of Virgo," "Embalming," "Terminal Moraine," "Inexorable," and others. In many ways, this book belongs to her…

For Nessie

Kestrel, Caifrân, Rónán
and Mum

TABLE OF CONTENTS

Tonight I've watched

The moon and then
The Pleiades
Go down

The night is now
Half-gone; youth
Goes; I am

In bed alone

– Sappho
Translated by Mary Barnard

ASTEROPE

ASTEROPE

I softly tread the shrouded wood
through the hallowed marrow of bone
beneath corrugated roots, these winter trees
suckle the light of stars long ceased to be

Photons falling through clouded thought
A god's great skull: the sky,
pierced by innumerable arrows
Only the head remains

to sing of silences sewn from dreams
of decomposing days

In amniotic fluids of decapitation
drift images concealed from time
by the tears of a mother,
a sister, searching such pooled waters
for lost flesh

Weep, oh Shining One, for the struggle
as synapses collapse
shattered stones once cradled
in a cranium broken
at birth, unable to suture
a self unknown

And yet, still I seek
in the reign of phoenix feathers
for the reverberations
of your living laugh
to grow as green shoots from
the mask of anonymous ash
becoming the numinous
bloom of light
in a sunset other than this

SMOKE + BLOSSOM

A flame-wrought silence
incomparably complete
renders my breath
profane. Still, I inscribe
the words of making
written as I walk
burning carbon in
tension
to acidic ash
baring wind-licked bones
blood erased and unencoded

I know nothing of peace lines
until twenty-five feet and four centuries
partition the darkness between me
and The Shankill

As the hail softens to snow
I should have known
that this moment would tease
the insatiable station
of parliament and pledges
to the final verge
urging the click
of a raptor's beak
as it breaks
delicate vertebrae
astray from burrows
sung as sinews wound
round roots keening deep
waters wrenched from
bedrock and the oak's beginning

I film the Easter snow,
a Belfast bleached before their birth,
but refuse to join the mob of mobiles

raised aloft hoping to catch
a TikTok Molotov

As naked
as the mouse exposed
to the dizzy oxidation
of unshackled sky –
vomiting from inversion –
and weeping
in a delirium that
writhes on the wrong
side of visibility,
a dark pillar ascends
authored by the abrasion
blurring each fictitious stratum

On the hill, spring's white blossoms unfurl
stark against the black smoke
of a burning bus

FALLING

Rhogam

Knowing
how dense a future
I had recklessly tethered
to the idea of you,
the doctor's voice sounds
genuinely relieved as he reads
the strength of the number
sampled at an hour
when tomorrow could be draped
in an unfounded hope
that dared to divide
and gestate
with such wild strength
that I choose
to explain away
the shift in a fibrous reality
slipping into blood

And I fail
to feel

anger at the injustice
as I wait
for the injection
to try to stop me
from killing you

Falling

When I could
no longer
hold you

        you
  t
  h   f
  r *me*
bod*y* l
  u   l   I'm so sorry,
  g
  h   he says,
               the levels are
               falling

            the numerical
code for death
audibly transcribed

the dissipation

of the cells
that would have been
stretched

further and further
into   I leave parts of
            you
in each hue
of the cotton spectrum of
my knickers, in the roots
of trees planted where none
should be, behind
the bleachers and between
the dugout and the roses
delineating the college boundary,
in the soft places of memory
and the bark of carparks

When I could
no longer
hold you

I lost
the only text
for the instructions
of your being
haphazardly bled
across the jurisdiction
of a notional geography

Running

The red of my inner thighs
reflects the russet rubber
of the track. I can taste
the uncomfortable confusion
of the collegiate male athletes
Even incomplete knowledge
of another's body is enough
to know that a period
can't last this long

I know I should look
each boy in the eye
with an almost smile
that speaks my lack
of shame
in the natural process
of my body shedding death

As if the mountain
would lower its gaze
when it fails to fill the river
or the salmon apologise
to the thousand eggs
it swallows

But I keep
my sunglasses on, eyes
transfixed by the white lines
leading me forward,
let the blood bead down my legs,
and keep running

Opened

I don't need
the lengthened waves
of the more expensive machine
to tell me how
swollen with death
the breath of you has become
when engorged on life

Those cells, until recently
so rapidly expanding,
have been drawing magnet-like
all vital fluids
to the site
of your unmaking

Where such a code
as was yours
is decomposing
in the centre of an ever-
diffusing universe

Without a big bang
there is only
a quiet falling

a part
of me knows
that the building pressure
and heat will burn
new atoms into
immeasurable existence
by splitting the old

So I rehearse
delivery:

lines to explain
how capable I am
of driving myself
from the radiology clinic
to the hospital
how safe

I thought our life
would undulate across
long lines of crayon and arguments
and blond hair turning
brown at almost fourteen
hours
they finally move
my bed from the emergency
department to pre-op

The unimaginable gravity
of a black hole
pulls all energy
into its longest possible form
until it approaches
the inobservable infinite

until all is shifted red

We have to wait
for the surgeon to birth
all the live babies before
she could end
the last of our mixed blood
by opening skin and muscle
and cutting you from
the place where we were one

She holds my hand
in the nova of anaesthetic
and afterward would tell
your father that you
had nearly begun
the universe anew

The density of your dying
slowed time

until mere minutes
remained before
I would have drowned
in the mattered expansion
of our burning blood

Days later I would be told
that the pathology department
had found your form
perfect in their division

I never granted permission
for anyone to touch you, to cut you

I don't know if I ever
had a choice
perhaps you became
hospital property
as soon as you were
removed from my body
still swaddled
in the tissues of my womb
I try not to think
of your small remnant
being incinerated with
the diverse detritus
of healthcare castoffs
changing state once again

from my need to your mass
from death to fuel to fission
to gas pulled into the longest light
by darkness

In the cooling before or after
the explosion in which
never-made elements
should congeal
I feel
the cold of 3 a.m.
and the empty space
of nuclei that didn't exist
enough to conjoin

and my arms ache
with the lightness
of never having held you

INEXORABLE

The many tongues
of the setting sun
grew as wings,
radials lashed by your radiance,
from my brittle back
as I walked away from you

From the memory of man,
the horn is shorn;
inexorable shards fall
in the trail traced between us

I speak only to the earth:
if any cracked rib
of conscience resides in her
to release you back to me

Or,
if she will not,
then to lick you gently
until you are
white

HALCYONE

HALCYONE

Bird,
bereft, sets adrift
a twig-plyed skiff
in days between
knowing and for
getting frost-blanked
baskets of ears
that cannot hear
the inconsolable ebb

You fold
into the fiction
of a pattern
pleated with
the storm-blown seed
of autumn

Rest the boats
beach-birthed
in the tempest
-uous knowledge
of a finite yearning
for a nest fallen
in the liquid leaves
of a spring's future

For the king within
the eggen belly to be
reaved by fire
air
rows the raven,
with oars less
                than
the collapsed ash
of the crownéd corpse
roaming on the sea
shells scattered

by the forested hull
woven from the
fibres of a year
by the hand of a whore

eyes on

the sinking
sun
that haunts
an unspeaking tongue
with deciduous
memories
shed

by pebbledash
tearing
fingertips
until the echo
of oceans
fade

BURIED

Aberfan, 1966

I wish I could mourn you:
anthracitic grief for my own
futility, as I stare
at the unsated river
beneath rusted blossoms
but my loss has been
buried in newspaper articles
and flowers lain by strange hands
in national indignation and the perfect
plaits of the other mothers

Some of whom have children still
and many more who soon will
We don't speak of it, don't lay hands
washed clean of the black sludge
fed by an umbilical spring unseen
and ask, "Are you trying?"

But when your father mines my body
I grind my teeth to drown
away the sound of the shovels
thrust again and again into the slag
unyielding

And as their bellies swell like the tip,
those mothers more fit than I,
who may yet wash small clothes
in the mouths of machines
quickened by the coal
that cost us our children
I know that I'm unworthy
Maybe if I had dug faster
if I had resisted
as Gransha pulled me away
if I had stayed
until I could see each bone
in my hands burnt bare

by the acid that ate
the flesh I built in my womb

We were unmade in a moment
not worn down by the slow
and gaseous years fingering
their way through porous stone
and I pray that the silken fibres
of your neck snapped
with a grace so fine time
couldn't register your existence

But though there is
no mark of you in this world,
save the lines
your loss branded
on my brow and the carbon
copy of your shadow
on my sightless irides,
you are irreplaceable

The redemption
your father seeks
to excavate within me
will not see a sunrise,
for, each month, I take a bus
to the city where they are illiterate
in the language that confesses
my skin scarred as
One of the Mothers

And there at the clinic they smile –
a pharmaceutical communion –
They swallow the unwritten lives
I tell them I can't
keep up with the ones I've already got
The lies come easily – I invent names
and ages and bicycle accidents –
I savour
what should have been ours

It is the image of you
dying alone that wakes me
in the night. Alone,
not fused like a child of Llŷr
to the brittle wings
of the deputy headmaster,
nor in my arms
where you should have been
and with faithless hands I grasp
at my wild and beating heart
beneath the slag heap of my breast
where milk will never flow again
and only black slurry remains

AMERICA

Potentialities
evaporate in the fluorine flicker
of a sun
whoreshipped by the shopper
as it drowns the fragile night
of annihilated archetypes
Corporate priests preside
over prophets predicting
the ebb and flow of the notional
Mark it
with the barcoded stigmata
of progress
replacing
darkness and poetry and my
lie nation

Inc.onstant indemnity shuns the
Other in this mass of shattered
bone and muscle
must sell
must
cell   (out)
of a collective prison
barred with chains of rewritten
Rotten**N**ationalist**A**merica

Mutate the membrane
to prevent the coiling of
constituents' chromosomatic choice
Hypo
might, oh   Chondria feeding
on Machiavellian misogynistic
masochism
in the schism
We subverted signs
to undermine the authority

But polysemic plurality was dis
solved by pandemic meaning,
momentary and untraceable

Etymological ephemerality
authored a single social narrative
idolized on glossy prints mass
produced to induce
waning thought
subsumed Instagra-
tifications of bite-sized
preruminated cognitions
Capitulating to the Glow,
we download
somatic suicide
as servants to the screen
in the radical exclusion of a centre
we sought to underwrite

The walls of the capitol castle have
been built with words we payed for
preyed for
Multiplicity blind to the bind
of unprecedented semiotic stability
fixed through the deletion
of all signifieds
in unparalleled poetic
Iron Ne
gating dreams of difference
in 50 ~~states~~ characters or less
Tweeting micro-meanihi
listlessness

COCONUT ICE CREAM

You comment on the quality
of the light and the vastness
of a sky unlike
the darkened
artex of the room
where you sit
for long and lampless hours
too tired to allow the scent
of clover to draw
those knotted bones – knitting
themselves down to the coming tide –
away from the work of forgetting,
pulled by the marionette strings
of a mourning you must renounce

The coming rattle foretells
the rhetoric of the
irreconcilable

Seated at the restaurant,
you ask again where we are
and the names of our children

I order for you
as I've become accustomed to doing
but I always get it wrong now
for the things
you once enjoyed have lost
their taste with their name

Ice cream
is the only thing you'll eat
They serve a single flavour here,
coconut, so I ask her to
bring it to you with the mains

Your frown
carves new graphemes
on an already furrowed face
as you feel the first flake
of unexpected flesh
on your tongue

Your apparent displeasure spreads
with the cracks of self and cirrus
streaming toward solubility
in the desert where,
sixty-seven years ago,
you followed the mirage
of a marriage your mother
told you to crave
and obeyed the airwaves
when the drought struck
and the radio
rationed each family
to one bath per day

You always insisted
I wash in the untouched water
and I pretended
that I didn't see you wince
as you rubbed my dirt
into your nakedness

I read again
that girl
in the text
of every fold

as you diligently remove
each desiccated shred
of coconut shrapnel
from the dish
I had chosen for you –
the one you had anticipated
to be smooth and clean
beneath the mercurial cream

TAGETE

TAGETE

Night-blooming mycelian
ground beneath the anxiety
of your first ungulae run,
long neck thickened
by the muscled will
of the ever-lockéd goddess
The forest strains
to stifle you
until slaked by
the fog-wreathed phallus
of his Olympian lust

You'd often wake
from swelling dreams
worried your son would
be born with hooves
and there in darkened certainty
you sculpted the river
of blood issuing from
an antler-torn placenta
that would fill once-living lungs,
between labour and lactation,
in the self-portrait of a corpse

Charon's depths obscured
the spartan tread
of the boy as he ran
the trigeminal topography
of a city
          stateless

Shed in the dissolution
of a son's sun
drowned
in the replication
of his rotting grandmother's
choice

to churn Acheron's
eschequered mire,
unmoored from life
by a hand too late
in knowing

the lanugo silk of his sister
pressed beneath
a patched and piecemeal
mothwing shroud

STILL LIFE OF VIRGO WITH COILED ROPE

My eyes,
cheap-ink facsimiles
of yours,
are spliced into
your coiled flesh,
nesting in the rope beneath
as you knot yourself, nearly
naked, around your knees

I watch the play
of light on the splay
of feathered vertebrae,
each shadowed valley
and ridge ringed
not with cloud
but car-shed soap,
a parallel reflection
of every turn in the twine

At thirteen, you are
yet caught in the
transcendent
tug-a-war of a body
about to transform

For now, you
are a field
of muscle flowing
from the centre
of that rope
wound round

you
emerging
from and into
the gravity
of so living a geometry

that the grass turns
to marsh gorged upon
the flaccid water falling
from my forgotten hose

For, in the pause be
twixt the touch of an in
candescent bubble
on the tall fescue
and its bursting,

the double
helix of your
bones tied
by guanine gauze
to the torqued
and twisting cord
is visible

And I feel
but cannot know
the acidic instructions
replicating enzymes
in me are en
crypted with a code
copied own^{lone}ly
in the com
pacting of us

so that we
are the double

cemented by
unseen centrioles
with a certitude
stronger than new
cleotides ebb

And the elegant
alleles of our in
dividual expressions,
bound as they are
beyond matter,
will remain mirrored
across time and space
and the lives we ply

EXPOSURE

Exposure Time: 1.333s

in

knock

Exposure Time: 3.2s

You
late

Before
it could

Exposure Time: 5s

Register
'nuther
police sightation

loitering

Exposure Time: 45s

palely twists
the viral code

unable

Two reproduce

Exposure Time: 1m 27s
slipping through
injection

(take me away from here)

Exposure Time: 4m 58s
Replica_shun
attainable only
through complete
Consumption

of the host

Exposure Time: 15m 37s
You can't kill
what's not alive

Exposure Time: 1h 25m
Car after car
flattens the discarded
ridges of the
caps
id
Io
sin cratic shattering
of a vitreous vacuole

There, on asphalt
made pliable
by unpredictable radiation,

scattered
in the shape of

an icosahedron
perpetually

rearranged

Exposure Time: 7d 19h

Each syringe siphons
the damaged
Daguerreotype of her DNA

in the exchange

A negative
never reprinted
despite
repeated exposures

Exposure Time: 3w 6d

Focused through
a legislative enlarger,
distributors publish an epi
dermic of
heliographic

Images burnt
by an unclaimed
sun

slowly fading

without a fix

Exposure Time: 4y 3mo.

There is no vaccine
for a society spiked
with parasitic predation

summoning
tumult
in the cyan flashing

of pictures
never illumined

Exposure Time: 12y 9mo.

half sick,
half shadow
I stop eating
reversing light and dark
in hypodermic delusion

my hands,
written by constructs
I didn't choose,
are not clean enough

to touch
anything that
enters my body

I am told that Exposure
Therapy is the only way
to counter the
obsessive compulsive wastage
of my corporeality

So I walk the streets
lingering in orange-cap
configurations

and persist in pretending
that my skin
cannot be pricked
by socially scripted
expectations

fearing the insertion
of conflicting helices

rather than admit
that choice
might be an illusion
precluded by the pattern
of proteins
shaping me

wishing not to recognize
that I am comprised
of photographic
philanthropy
stitched from three
trillion vulnerable cells
behind
vacuous membranes

Exposure Time: 20y

With an audience
of those who pass in cars
and see unwatching

She washes her hair
in the tub
her dog
drinks from

Cracke
d
ecaying
in vein

by nuanced
and needled
rupture

Exposure Time: 45 y

Opiate and virion
suspended in the volatile
solute of the once
deliquescent mark

Silver salt

made visible
by copper
washed with
dreaming blood

and stripped
by light

TERMINAL MORAINE

I shook with the fever of a locked door
but the absence of my forfeited key
reminded me that this
was not my home
anymore. The frame rattled
with a hollow mockery
echoing through our ice-licked
valley once torn into being
by water that walked through land

I should have remembered
what locked doors looked like
when I screamed at the doctor
to give breath
to the body cadenced by machine
as I bargained with fluorescence and iodine
to rewrite the rise and fall
of the monitor's mountains and valleys

****

The sigh in which a glacier begins to die
is marked by a terminal moraine,
a final extremity of existence
recorded in the language of stone
debris and boulder balanced in a
desperate whisper over aeons:
once I was here

Tremors of forgetting
revert the glacier
to a futile liquid
consumed by the land
it once erased

And sometimes I can hear
the inherent fragility of the ice
crack in the ecstasy
of relinquishment

CELÆNO

CELÆNO

He burned me
with a fire stolen
from languishing gods
too distracted by inde
fatigable envy to
inhabit the silent
space between an ember's
final quenching
and the rising of
a separate smoke

But death is too pure
for indistinct intentions

He anointed my shoulders
with the dark patterns
of stars swallowed by
titanic stone dying
to a world become
and in the ground
charcoal of now cold flame
he branded not a claim
but an acknowledgement
of sight
in that place
before light

And I knew in the want
of his blackening mark
beneath that text older
than time
he was driven by
a desire deeper than
my need for skin

In his Promethean pride
of the shoulders
others had tried to hide
I knew too
it would be only he,
for only an exiled god
could coax the canid and chimeric
from this body earth-bound

SHEDDING

It was not rebirth
written into the laboured
breath of sloughed skin,
but the seven doors
of Ereshkigal's realm con
tracting, teasing tensions into
Inanna's nakedness
I too was being stripped
and as the dust
of depleted DNA
clung to my eyebrows it
clogged each flustered follicle
until pustules poured the pattern
of who I might have been
Da Vinci would have drawn me
as a shade of humanlike
Kafka's creatures courting inclusion

The doctor warned
that my body would
consume its own heart
if I continued
this diet of penance
and toxic fumes
but still I emptied
C_3H_8O by the hour onto
the face I was erasing

And as I scrubbed
with cotton bud the slurry
of selves stretched
over a frame of diverse lives
I counted the fading
cadence of indiscernible
endings

The theory of an under
active preorbital cortex
was tattooed on the vellum
of a wasted life
Rational observers questioned:
can't they see their own potential?

But Jocasta's brooch was in a bottle,
so I bought blindness for my ~~birth~~day
In splitting the perverse
caduceus: Tiresias was trans
formed, not eye
washing away the final barrier
with the milk-white tears
of the snake before
it slips into the new

In releasing the imprint of each
irreplicable scale I knew
I would not have a skin beneath
to conceal that knotted muscle
in its obstinate rhythm

BLODEUWEDD

The sun of another
continent's sky
was projected through
the fog fractals
of my reversed night
as I slid
the superlative lock, heavy
with subterfuge
and silicon encased,
from the place
where it rested between
the blackened aluminium
of forest and football field

When first I heard
the call, I thought
it but a single bird
beating its barbéd dirge
from tree to leafless tree
and I thought of you,
a teenage Blodeuwedd,
and how royally Guest
had fucked the story up

Your feathers,
the way they tell it,
began

an abrupt
rupturing
from within
as sow supped
maggots from the wounds
of expectations
you were formed
and fashioned
to fulfil

the ones you left
to hang among
the barren branches
as larvae fell
from putrid lives

But your skin
was smooth
when you died
(the undertaker didn't
say nuthin' 'bout 'avin
to pluck you)
so I think it was
the wrong bird
transformed

For your flight
was not from what
you should have been,
nor even
from moss-grown boy
to man

but from an in
finite chain
of amino acids
balanced on a back
bone drawn by a wizard
with a Crayola on stone
pierced
by a black
whole, spilling:
milky ways to spell and sell
your name
carved in cardiac
equation to theirs
a J on one oak
and an A on

another owl
bends to fill itself
with the unnervingly warm
nocturnal air
as it breaks
its dialogue with the
bird I cannot see

But I know
it flies above me
as I force broken
nails through barken
rifts to find

letters etched eight
years ago by a blade
bent in a high school
shop class by a boy
I watched put a ring
on a fluid-filled finger
after life and lover
had left you

I thought
the remaining owl
might cease its song
in solitude
but as I searched
for the sap-sutured cipher
the tone
of the lone bird's questioning
swelled into the emptied
acoustics of the woods
until it occurred to me
that what I sought
had never been written
and all I could hear
were toads and
the plaintive critique
of voiceless cars
on pavement across the river

DEEP SPACE OBJECT

E
I wonder what is hidden
beneath the polyester
tablecloth starched
in a concrete block basement
at unsociable hours
by hands from elsewhere,
no more linen than my hair
is still chestnut beneath
its chemical dye

But there is comfort
in the artificial,
in effortless forms manufactured
Seventeen months from now
we will drink cheap chardonnay
from a BPA-free Eddie Bauer
knockoff Nalgene bottle
beside a river reeling
as it falls
from mountain grace

Yet, its soft sedimentality
will be indistinguishable
from the crinkle of the
plastic packaging encasing
coupled biscuits
individually wrapped

And though the snow slated
to become that river
has neither fallen nor melted
I think I already have
the memory of Mint Milanos
in my mouth as I watch you
laugh at my unfunny jokes

and grip your glass' slender stem
to keep your hand from shaking
The hand that will in one hour
and thirty-seven minutes be warm
for the first time on the cold catch
of my trousers

For here in this very moment
of beginning, the death
of distant stars
is dissolving all we do,
our bodies slowly open
with a serrated steak knife
bare against the bleach

M

I decide not to tell you
that today we mapped
an unnamed
deep space object

Its existence remains
theoretical despite the finite
prick I plotted,
constant and visible,
on the grid of our screens

We were able to extrapolate
its location only through
a lack of light, the possibility
of space impenetrable
to photonic activity

Perhaps I don't want
to acknowledge that
if the sun of an unseen
system incalculably far
from the twice refinanced
new build on Ashwood Lane

can be comprised of
absence alone
so could lesser things

C²

I will refuse to name
the anti-matter
of that distant
and inanswerable ache
to exist

Thus, in our refusal
we will orbit
the kitchen island cut
from Daltile granite look-a-like
(c.f. comfort in artificiality)
with the already-dead
dust of our wanting
diffuse and dying in our
need

For the midden of our dark marriage
is not substantial enough
to produce a gravitational pull
and, knowing my unspoken
deep space object (I wonder, did you
read the article I left in the basket
beside the settee?) is – despite its number –
no matter,
we speak of anything
but the speed of separation

accelerating
toward an end
of light and gasses
unbound from one and
[sm] Other so
completely that act
(d)ual emptiness

is rendered
in the wake of
fragments

exonerated
by that final explosion
unmade
as the mémoire of mutual
atoms shared
is incinerated

ELECTRA

ELECTRA

Shore-scattered amber
is ground by the dark
sand of a Slavic shingle
where half-integered Harpies
roost on wreathéd rocks
above the sea-sculpted basin
of absent fathers
flushed in the flow
of forgetting

Rewired by
the Trojan ghost
of the old king's gold
as alloy
in a bed
blood soaked by
murder and men
Stray shone
Orestes' electron
of ladies most deject and wretched
who, behind a thinly veiled
virginity, vowed in the frac
tallied fermions of
Agamemnon's arteries
to never

become
the mother

BIRЄ^{T}H

I: Follicle Stimulation

Icanthus incantations
can't loosen
the locks of the long-dead
soldiers slain in claiming
this stretch of Baltic dirt

Darkly peated,
pleated beneath
the skeleton stalks of wheat
less numerous
than the silenced dreams
and brick-red thoughts
of a tomorrow removed

Copses of birch
(as black and white as my need for you)
flank a clay-baked castle
blooded crimson
in this bleached landscape
linking each luteal phase
to the lunacy
of a language that
can't be born

wordless
it stitches
the folds of a viscous mantle

As cracked and faulted
as I am, I cannot escape
as vapour or ash or stone
I'm grasped by powdered bones
that say, "what choice had we?"

The shadowed power
of each brick bought
with the only rook-baited
currency they had to barter
cannot blacken the leucious grain
even when the turrets block the moon

Sliding the cap from the twenty-sixth syringe
I'm reminded of those spires
and hope an errant cow
grazes wantonly
on the wheat of the dead,
threshing the chaff of those
whose such repose
know not how I dig
the fleshy earth above
plow need by need[le]
deeper into the loam
of my stomach

With a surgeon's care, I angle the drug
so as not to penetrate the wordlessness
watch it map a scarlet territory
through the conquest of battles lost
by my inability to construct
simple chains of common hormones
and know that I cannot mimic
the words of the murdered

II: Implantation

My feet, healed in sterility,
can create
nothing
but shallow air
at less than cosmic angles
from my hips
where the only waves
                                are ultrasonic

When I look at them there
on the screen
– those perfect circles of cells –
I see the amber glow
of the urge for life

preserved in seeming stone
of crystalline sap once
viscid when ancient
crania were still forming

Tapped by speculum on catheter
those electric cells slide
into the carefully measured
space within me
I try to breathe away
the heave of tears
but notice when I rise
that the paper is wet

The birch bark
roll of the Baltic
wraps my tongue
in thoughts of quiet thunder
sculpting sands
where hopes are shored
of cries to come
flighted from murmuring pines
in the wind's answer

this desolation is my glory
until even my defects
are made translucent

I cradle the symmetry
of a barnacled skull
and in walking break
what the sea had spared

But it is many miles
before I see the rounded sheen
of millennia's blood
bled into the sap of would
now rafter to the waves
the old ones darken
fifty million years
twisted into the guanine
of the gem laying light
in the pubic weed
of Kolka's lost
Livonian sand

where the first mother lay
on a seabed of amber
when, from six eggs,
five embryos grew in a dish
as she pushed these lands
from the ankled furrows
of her birth throes
beneath a sky
half egged and unbemused

III: Gestation

Balanced as Lleu
between slipping amnion
and dry stone
I am rocked into
a cochlear spiral

as I watch
the sun set
on the remains
of a year that slides
from the caress
of coiled intestines

An uncanny heat
makes the blood beat
in a swollen song
from foetus to foetus
the sleeping tongue
between life and life
that they will never
speak again

once light has sanctified
a separation
beneath a Beltane
as of yet unwritten

when open eyes erase
the triple-hearted time
possibilities curl, unexploited,
in the shifting place
where earth coalesces
in the skinless air above
the river where the dog's gaze,
keen and knowing, is fixed
on the submerged father

And the current will pull
me on to the haemorrhaged
hour of our meeting:
beneath my belly
you are becoming
exponentially more
than my need or his anxiety

Myriad lives
unfold and shift
from the darkness in me

My scar-stretched skin,
muscle roped long by progestin,
and my most desperate fears
will not be able to protect you
then

The world will open you
in beautiful and tragic and unseen creation

as you fold yourselves
in two shapes unknowable, distinct

gnawing the spear-struck
hole in the stone
of my calcified chest
through which
you'll flow

IV: Partum
I mourn already
the moment I cannot reach
for your foot within me
as it billows the surface of my belly
breeching from a secret sea

fleetingly, before, cooled by the newness,
it slips beneath once more

I want to memorize
each silk-skin movement
each roll and protrusion
knowing that this
is the last night

you will ever
swim within me
breathing our tripartite fluid

in meeting tomorrow
the hollowness of air
I hope the lightness of it
will not leave you feeling empty

What inobservable dance
will ever speak between the limbs

of you
    two who have shared be
                                    coming

I will decorate the winding myelin
of my brain and the heart
that beat for three with the
cells you leave behind

I wonder if my nipple
will feel rough in your mouth
having known only dark and liquid
lungfulls

Will I taste the bitter drum
of my uterus on your skin?

The flood of your shedding
as I lay bitchlike,
panting
will mark the cumulative
moment of every expansion,
from the first hydrogen
unfolding in newly made heat
to the great swell
of my soon slackened stomach,
and every contraction,
from palaeolithic orgasm
to the push that will
give you yourself

And the only way
I'll be able to bear it
will be to find
your face at my breast
when in the vastness of space
only we will exist

in all of time unfurled and unfurling
just us, now parted

ILMARINEN

Coniferous in
sense
coats the air

Common words to right
the axis of attachment
are charred on shards
scattered as ruins
to foretell the soliloquies
of sirens ensoiled
as they circle
matrices of trees
sighing in consentric rings
to enform human flesh that
living time is correlated

Falling through a femur
the bone dance pulls you
into a meadow moon bedewed

Stick-slipped eddies stir
the uneasy bile
of rock-strewn River
Mortis' relenting waters
sieved by the one who bore
such a lean Lappish lad

When the hooves
of the snow-forged
revealed iron
it was consecrated
in the carbon
of the bear's blood

You saw
pattern-welded atoms
studied the folds

until you could
replicate the bond
in stalactites
of saliva hung
between thumb
and sternum

until you could call
the name of the haemorrhage
to bind sage and semantics and semen
in dark flame flung
from a far star

only then, refined
could you create the *sampo*
in the thicket of your thalamus

and in forgetting fall
from the known
finding the
inconvenient actuality
of a ground by gravity governed

where you carved
the boned material of self
and in making
made a god

GUðRÚN

"Melancholy – fear of aphanisis – punctuated
by sudden bursts of energy
marks the loss of the maternal body,
this immediate investment of sadism in the symbolic."
– Julia Kristeva, *The Severed Head*

I

I collected class rings
hoarded from each hand
that unzipped my jeans
hammered from disappointment;
I sucked fingers
until I could taste bone

Through the dragon haze
of Chico's joint
Sigurd sighs in the
absence of her ice-clad body
as he pictures penetrating
that perfection, scattering pearls
from Daddy lavishly wound to hide
the tracks of unspoken
runes

Between dream
and frozen sword,
she may have his love
but I have other gifts

I offer him a consoling
smile and plastic cup
of cheap vodka and Pepsi
red and brittle
with transience. In sharpie
I scrawl *Sigurd Serpent Slayer*

When he is least himself
I unlace
padded football pants,
stained with grass and frat boy hopes
straddling the blade
he was saving for her

II

We married when
there could be no denying
my distended abdomen
for I wanted all my mother's
friends to know
I would never
be good enough for her

Sigurd would leave
when the baby cried
and, returning to a rain
of ceramic shards,
he would say only
that he had been driving

My mother often told me
not to shout at the child
forgetting as she fondled
her little prince
the screams recorded on
the soundtrack of my childhood

My son ate only Taco Bell,
Mac 'n Cheese,
and cold hot dogs from the can
for in my refusal to cook
I would prove
I was not like her

Some nights
I would turn the tap
on the tub too high
trying to scald
away the vocabulary
of rejection
The boy, bathed in
the dragon's blood,
would cry as I
clawed at my skin
to slough my flawed
scales
until they fell
in drowned
constellations
to sink in the shape
of a life in which he loved me
like so many purgatorial petals
painting my womb-fashioned replica of that hero
down to the small red bud

And after I failed
to smelt our insufficiencies
I would run an obligatory comb
through the child's wet hair
as he sat in jim-jams and genes
that did not match
But when he whined in pain
as I pulled at the tangled mess,
I would break the brush
on the seven sections
of the now-sutured skull
that once tore me
until he learned
to never say it hurt

III

When Sigurd died
it looked like an accident
I think my grief
was the only reality
I have felt – to forfeit
what had been
so carefully stolen
Because I'm easily replaceable
I gave the boy to my mother
on an autumn day
stripped
of wanting
and boarded a plane to Europe
with a cumulonimbus of possibility pressing
on my clitoris
in a stirring more tangible
than his distracted fingers
ever were

I was worshiped
in a ruined Greece
with the fragility
of a cicada's wing
mounted on marble
ground with each thrust
to limestone dust
blown with the seeds
of impotent pillars slick
with the oil of a million
unwanted fingerprints

With temples
throbbing each sanguine sunrise
I drank
and fucked my way north
through an Italian mosaic of men:
Robertos, Andreases, and Fabrizios interlocked

around my limbs
in pools haunted
by the memory of water
reduced
by the tread
of two thousand years
to dis
        connected fragments

But it was in Paris
that I met my next husband
behind a door
on the Champs-Élysées
that slid back to reveal
privilege concealed from day

Attila, hun,
grey for my flesh,
leaned languidly
against the upholstery of a booth
that could only be bought

IV

I liked the way he said my name
– though it sounded like Goose Run – and overlooked
the pimp-like gold
chain around his neck
binding
as I became his whore
dead
chalice

A goblet
supersaturated in semen
twice swelling with sons

V

When they were maybe four and five,
my brother Gunnar
came to visit his nephews
Attila drew him in
as Sigurd never had

On a night humid with August escapism
the men ventured into a city sans Parisiennes
The boys were laughing with their nanny
as I gloated in the champagne of my superiority:
how easily Gunnar, mother's soul treasure,
had been enchanted
by Attila's glamour

It wasn't a noise that woke me
but some form of knowing
that drew me stick-figured
stalking up stairs
I never strode

Our building boasted
a ghosted garret
where families forgot
the stories of their excess

I heard groans
he never made for me
and still it took time
to recognise my husband's back
engulfing a small form
with outstretched
wings pinioned beneath
his forearms as he slowly
drove himself within

It was then I saw Gunnar
in the yellowed streetlight

grinding below Attila
mounted on his mare

Because they had not heard me,
occupied as they were,
I was able to
inaudibly retreat

In the masquerade
of his Magyarhood,
Attila kept a ceremonial sabre
LED lit in the display case
behind his desk

My hand felt as though
it had always fit the hilt
with such ecstatic intensity
that it dispelled any revulsion –
any premature sorrow –
for the deed I was
about to commit

Sealed by steel
it was the inevitable culmination

I laid the blade
at the foot of our bed
before rousing the children
Sleep with me?
I asked
Mummy's had a bad dream

The older boy wrapped his arms
around my neck
in sleepy reassurance
as I carried him
followed by his brother

VI

I made certain to be sitting
serenely at the table
with a book and composure
when, reeking and raucous,
Attila and Gunnar returned

I couldn't sleep,
I told them sweetly

And I thought you might
be hungry,
so I fixed some food

Attila made a joke
about how he didn't
think I knew
where the kitchen was
and Gunnar grumbled his agreement
before collapsing on the couch

Mon mari
sighed his satisfaction
This meat is so yielding, he said
pulling me onto his lap,
that I don't need a knife

Attila, beloved, sauced in the
silenced honey of our hearts
it is the very tenderest

MEROPE

MEROPE

Wisdom, tinted yellow
by the pollen-dusted
nipples of eloquence,
led Sisyphus to surrender
to the mead-sweet mér
opium of ultra
violate sight

in the flight
that melted a hymen
op tear a

Mellifera maddens
the hand tracing a
hunter blinded by a
hamulic huntress

Trading gold for brass
the armoured thorax
of the Bee-Eater is
reflected in the Oedipal
glâs, a facet of Glaucus the Drowned
see God
in the gleam
of a honied seem
men by ommatidia masked
in the mud beneath
the hoof of a mayor
chained in the office
of forgetfulness

The polarised pupil
is punished by a prophet
probing the triangulation
of oracular ocelli

Isolating those procl-
aiming all drones
beaten by white canes
in supplication to the black
who shook the seven
spots into the grey
Temple de l'Oublie

EMBALMING

They warned us 'bout fluids,
forbade us to touch you
until Adam had filled your quiet
veins with his substance

Mother roared by the gas fire
to the woman
in the merchandizing
showroom of caskets
that no man would put his hands
and more
within your naked flesh

So I was sent
to clothe your exposure
Ma will never know
how late I was,
how many hands had carved
with intention, scalpel, and prick
furrows upon the fallow
field of your belly

I can trace each incision
upon the protest
of my tongue,
plot the large and useless
sutures
hastily tied
with the pretence
of putting you back together
(not like our father's close
 and careful work to mend
 the asphalt bite
 when you fell off my bike)

Pints of plasma
weighed heavily
in your listless limbs
as I shouldered long legs
Lace underwear
could not obscure
those sprawling gashes
The jeans refused, though I insisted
But the most difficult dressing
was to lift your torso to entangle
your chest with a bra
(though you hardly needed one)

I failed in my task
and sent you unclasped
to the timelessness below the soil;
beneath your new plaid shirt
no one will know

I left you to Adam then,
but I do not think he did his work
for as you lay displayed
in Ma's sun room
I watched new patterns
arise on your checked shirt
and rolled back your sleeve
to wipe away the blooming blood
as I had done
when we were young

at my touch your decay
-ing epidermis
gilded my palm
as your skin
came away with mine

I should have cut
a strip of flesh
from my own arm

for there were gaps
as I tried
to puzzle
each patch
so recently you
back into position

until I begged
Ma to let you sleep
safe in dark dignity

Now, outside the bleating
spring is laughing
as lambs fall and I murmur
across those years:
Live with me

For in days that draw me
further from you
I married a museful man
So I know
the things of life
that killed you now
and he don't need Ma's permission
to embalm me
It is warm on my fingers
where once your blood
was cold and dark

PENELÓPE

I attempt to summon
to my mind the man
who will wear your work
I wonder if he appreciates
your hands

What spells of protection
do you will into your wool
to warm the family
without my name
Your feet move between
heddles
illiciting a dull moan
when they meet

Imagined milk
whitens whorlds
diffuse and darkened
by a soluble sheath
of fibre spinning forward
fleeting, bleating, into
nothing
but the tangled
yarn of roots
dyeing the spring soil

Does a space exist
for the weft to tra–
verse within
shed the skin shuttling
sensation binding bundles
of dumb nerves
warps run as vertebrae
silenced without my fingers
forbidden to tune the forgotten
bone

I leave you at your loom
to your husband and your cloth
From fibres of chaos
you have created text
stiles I hurdle as I pick my way
through field and injustice,
staring at the creatures
whose fleece you have fashioned
flattened and defined
and think how lovely
lamb will taste tonight

Voyager I

You knew
before we
began
that we

would part

Both
our lenses
metacognito
obscura

Ergo obtentus

Knowing
en absentia
our soles would
diverge, print *primera*,
at the foot
of a never
imagined volcano

A false heat
r o l l i n g

as intractable
as Jupiter's
quarantined gases

Each insoluble part

unable to touch

what is beside

We, knew,
our end
was in the middle

Voyager II

I could detect
my mother's pleasure
when she told me

my sister
had seen you
kissing
someone else

Each weak[end]
pulse

I decide
to walk
a new traged
E°ctory
around the places
we would linger
to avoid

the fallen quanta
of time bent
to suit
forced fission

Each moon,
the passing
images recon
structed on a
sterile screen,

I calm
myself to sleep
with unhapp
end scenarios

in which you turn,
unscripted, from your
quest beyond
this star,
my detail,

of these drear spheres

I don't

want
to trans[ad]mit

mis

Inter

per

able data

That know g

we
re
wa

…t

Re:
Re
al

… made it

So,
I

…us

confessing your
numerically coded mis
Take
a picture

when you are alone

I can imagine
a space of
particles so sparse
that you forget
the revolving system
behind

In iso*l*ation only
can you move
(beyond these unceasing
orbits)
for any mass
when too close
can solely circle

It grows to the light,
you once said
in a lavender drone
that you had never felt
this close to anyone
too near to see that we
were entwinned by vines choking
each other in their desire to seek
the sun

I can possess
the first eye in the universe
to see within the russet crevice
but I cannot comprehend
that you exist
still unclaimed
by death's obliteration
and live a life
without me

MAIA

MAIA

The flesh
tears so easily
beneath
parallel pleats,
claw-ploughed,
and seeded
with the possibility
of knowing

Vaporous and
without guarantee,
disquieting dreams stream
from prophetic seams
taunting sacred
skin: from chert-
cracked crevice
to cervical solitude
the Vulcanic mountain
still rises
through troposphere
to rend a
shallow sky

But quiet
are the dales of Arcady
where wild Arcas
was wont to roam
wearing the mask
of Callisto's curse in
                                                ursa
Mine or hers
I could not discern
the outline of
my bear body
from the forested
scent of his fur

and the hot fall
of blood where
his teeth tore
my teats
as he nursed

WREN

In the warp of your wing
there is woven a text
authored by Aeolus
spun round the shaft
of each feather, barred
equally with dark and with light,
inked in the disintegration of stars
falling over each of your eyes
lured by the illusion of space
when a glass lie
broke your bones of air
on the shortest day of all
when the North,
tired of being read in the sun,
speaks to the black
where nothing can be scripted
Not you wrenovatio
nor the nebulae breathing away
from the mass of meaning
mouthed by the gravity
that brought you to ground,
set your neck at twenty-three degrees
So we hatched you
in a nest of rosemary
upon whose branches blossom
blue novae inhaling
to recompose galaxies
we once thought written

THE RIFT

North American Plate
Concealed by five hundred
generations of moss,
the unspoken testament
to metamorphosis stilled
is compressed by my specificity

Gravity is less severe this far north
A scent of citrus pervades
a wind to which it does not belong,
prevailing dreams of ignoble progress
from left and right converging

Continents devouring each other
in a Richter scaled ritual
rent by breath to raise
a dialogue of at most fear
Said a menstrual stratum
lying to mount and birth
and pull a part
ing of an inch each
millennium in
the sabotage of separation
undone on other borders

Walking awhile with what remains
of a sheep, bone white
in this trench not yet of tears
A flower for my living sister
and one for the other
as I write the names of the dead
in the youngest rock on earth

The crowberries stain
my fingers a feast for corvids
as I carve a sandcastle
from crumbled crystal cast
aways in this rift unscarred
by glacial prede lick
shun sun and stone
feeding a sea that covers
all that time and tectonics
cannot erase

Eurasian Plate
Two pale flowers,
one for my dead sister
and one for my live,
broke the heather held
by moss generations deep

A smell of lemon borne
on an Arctic wind
caused me to pause as such
singular citrine scent defied limits
to roam, a stark and invasive censer

A crow well-kept watched me –
death is larger and deeper here
Mímirs eyed unblinking as I lay
the effigies of children not yet born to sleep
causing the insubstantial to stir amidst
trails of contractions and trials of fault
lines walked by the unseen
in mounting pressure to break
beneath the wait of a planet
breathing bright blood
through the porous progress of bone

I found Aurore tied below
the centuries of twisted branches
abandoning sky to grow close to earth
Listening to the magma smouldering still,
I kneel to the forgotten song revere
berating in hollow spaces held by basalt
to drink that discarded breath

For I will drown
in this trough of milk, the artery
that breeds all dark and dreaming spaces
and fertilizes tectonic trenches traced to separate,
some by ocean filled and some containing
the gaseous mist that quenches scent
and memory where drifts
the dust of pollen and predation
that intermingle in the descendants
of a monohued meteor

ENTANGLEMENT THEORY

Alone,
I drink
stratospheric vapours
from a glass lens
fluted in an observe a
(s)tory trans
scribing
a distant planet in
verbatim dictation
conveyed through the semaphore
of villi folding
hydrogen and helium,
breathing Helios' secret sign

And I am no more
than carbonic tissue
and graphite bartering
phonemes for photons
falling through millennia
to set me ablaze
in darkened entrenchment

entangled particles
will ever
compose the other

But as my mitochondria
burn the breath
of extinct gravities
I know that the spectral print
of a sun enumbered
makes visible a hemisphere

too tangibly to steel
the fading embers
of a name
forgotten before its birth

Enearthed in exhalation
I look again through the telescopes
shuffling a symphony of com–
promises
and see
the dark matter
of our viscera
in the inverted images
of the
stars

NOTES ON THE POEMS

"Buried" was previously published in *The Seventh Quarry* Vol. 28 (2018)

"America" was previously published in *The Seventh Quarry* Vol. 28 (2018); *Genre: Urban Arts* (2019); *Still: The Journal* (2019); and *West Trade Review* (2019)

"Exposure" was previously published in *The Seventh Quarry* Vol. 28 (2018) and *Sand Hills Literary Journal* (2020). If a negative is overexposed in the dark room, the unique and unrecoverable images contained on it are burned into oblivion. Less of the poem is visible as it progresses and becomes overexposed to demonstrate the burning away of the subject's identity the longer she is unhoused – the longer she is exposed. The narrator is a separate individual who is undergoing Exposure Therapy for OCD triggered by the syringes that connect them to the unhoused subject. The exposure times above chart both photographic processing and the subject's length of time being unhoused and are initially exposure times within normal photographic limits for the differing processes of negative preparation and printing exposures (some historical processes are referred to with longer exposure times); however, these times become stretched, as the poem is itself, beyond what is survivable.

"Shedding" was previously published in *The Seventh Quarry* Vol. 28 (2018)

"Bire^{t}h" The first part of this poem charts the Welsh narrator's experience receiving fertility treatment in the Baltics. In *Icanthus*, I am blending *Acanthus* – a plant associated with life, death, and regeneration – with Welsh "canu" (to sing – in this case to sing into creation in a mythic sense) and echoing I can/I can't, suggesting both limitation and potential in relation to the fertility treatment and asking what creation means when sought so deliberately. Leucious is meant to reflect milk (the colour and breastfeeding context) and describe the very pale colour of dried wheat in terms of leucism, whilst still connecting it to the yellow-hued luteal phase of the menstrual cycle.

"Merope" Halumic links the anatomical with the hamuli of the bees' wings associated with Merope as bee-eater bird, and the multifaceted eyes of insects evoke the blindness in the myth.

"Embalming" was previously published in *Cheval 7* (2014)

"Penelópe" was previously published as "Woman Weaving" in *Cheval 6* (2013)

"Inexorable" was previously published as "Inexorable Shards" in *Cheval 5* (2012)

ACKNOWLEDGEMENTS

Thank you to the authors, publishers, and translators whose work has been briefly quoted under fair use, including Sappho, Mary Barnard, Julia Kristeva, and Jody Gladding.

I would like to thank Aida Birch, Alan Perry, and the Cheval team for their efforts to inspire young Welsh writers through the Terry Hetherington Young Writers Award – your work is invaluable. Likewise, Peter Thabit Jones has been instrumental in hosting the AmeriCymru Prize.

My gratitude is due to Todd, Cate, and Amira at Black Spring Press Group for their vision, patience, and flexibility as this manuscript became a book and to Christopher Jackson for believing in it. Dr Zoë Brigley brought insight, depth, and clarity to the work in the early editorial process, and Andrew Sullivan was a keen draft reader. Professors Kevin Mills, Bob Lyman, and Charlie Thomsen, you have all helped to shape me and this book.

Amie, Shosha, and Elena, thank you for being chosen sisters in my star cluster, and Kiki you are my irreplaceable guardian light. Mum, thank you for being my first scribe and hearing my words when no one else could. I love you $(I_{\circ}I)^{I} + I$... Shane, thank you for writing this story with me.

Finally, I would like to thank Kessie, Cai-Cai, and Rónán for playing pirates, loving words, and collecting letters as we got this book to the printers. I love you more than all the stars in all the galaxies in all the universes.

www.ingramcontent.com/pod-product-compliance
Ingram Content Group UK Ltd.
Pitfield, Milton Keynes, MK11 3LW, UK
UKHW012115131225
466037UK00003B/84